Highlights

Hidden Pictures

EASTER PUZZLES DELUXE

tomatoes

HIGHLIGHTS PRESS
Honesdale, Pennsylvania

Wild Flower Wanderings

spoon

button

wishbone

horseshoe

bell

banana

 ball of yarn

hairbrush

loaf of bread

 sock

 piece of candy

It's wild flower season, and the hills have come alive with color.
Can you find the hidden objects among the flowers?

Art by Paula Bossio

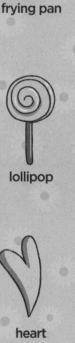

fork

frying pan

lollipop

heart

fish

candy cane

glove   scissors   pencil   yardstick   seashell

Robo Rabbit

Carrot, please! See if you can find the hidden objects around these rabbit friends.

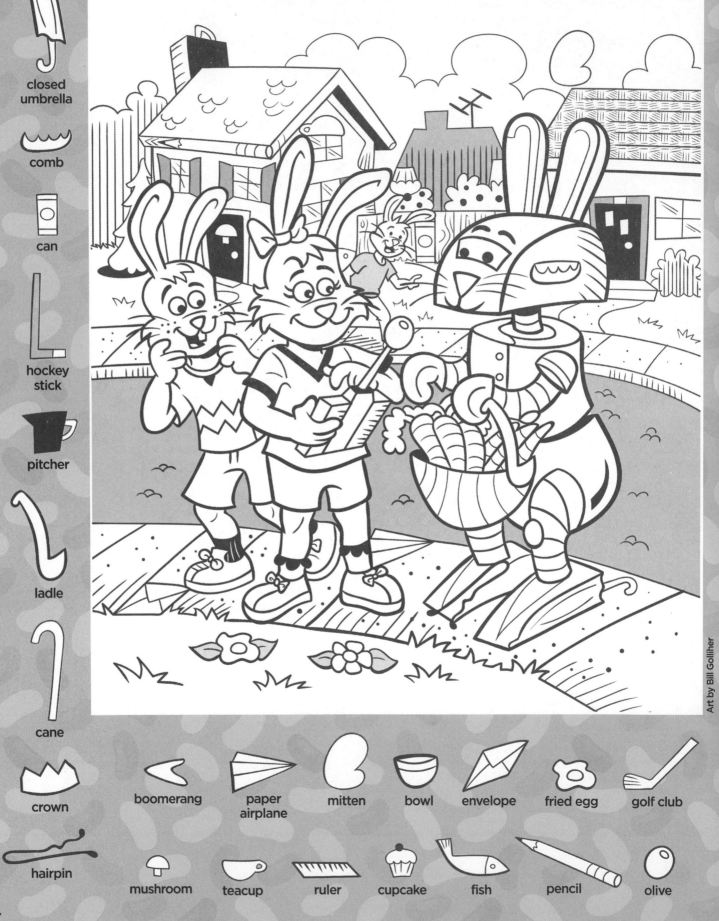

closed umbrella

comb

can

hockey stick

pitcher

ladle

cane

crown

boomerang

paper airplane

mitten

bowl

envelope

fried egg

golf club

hairpin

mushroom

teacup

ruler

cupcake

fish

pencil

olive

Art by Bill Golliher

In the Coop

Can you find at least 10 differences between these two pictures?

Art by Jackie Stafford

5

Take Two

Each of these scenes contains 12 hidden objects, which are listed below. Find each object in one of the scenes, then cross it off the list.

Art by Julissa Mora

banana	comb	heart	pencil
baseball bat	crescent moon	hockey stick	ring
bell	crown	mitten	ruler
broccoli	envelope	mug	slice of pizza
button	fish	nail	sock
canoe	fork	needle	worm

Ants on Parade

Hip hip hooray! It's parade day in Ant Town. Can you find the hidden objects?

lollipop

fishhook

baby's bottle

broom

pencil

artist's brush

coffeepot

fried egg

banana

bell

sock

ruler

Art by Patrick Girouard

8

Bunch of Bunnies

Can you find the squirrel?
Can you also find 12 hidden acorns?

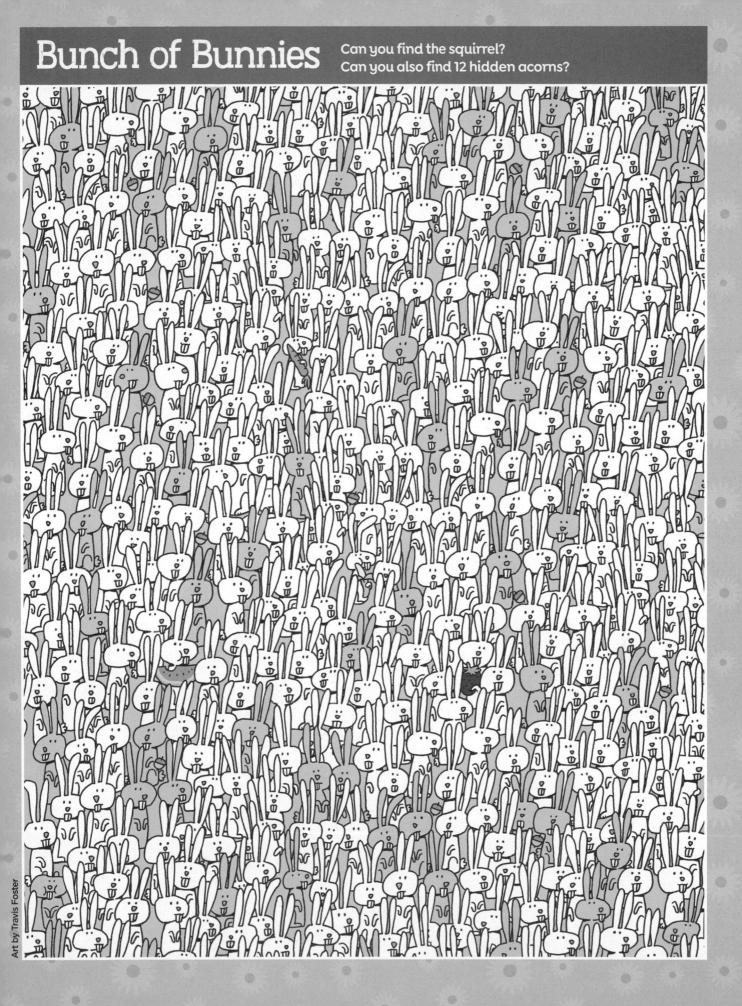

Art by Travis Foster

Bird Buddies

baseball bat

candle

scissors

ruler

slice of pizza

party hat

fan

belt

hamburger

ring

envelope

wedge of lemon

ball of yarn

fish

toothbrush

10

All the birds are saying hello on this lovely spring day.
See if you can find the hidden objects around the birdhouses.

snake

carrot

frying pan

kite

magnet

crescent moon

lollipop

fried egg

teacup

wristwatch

mitten

saw

dog bone

comb

Art by Mernie Gallagher-Cole

11

Bunny Birthday

flag

wristwatch

needle

slipper

acorn

snake

bell

domino

nail

ring

**It's Rachel Rabbit's fifth birthday!
Can you find the hidden objects at the bunny party?**

pennant

ghost

sailboat

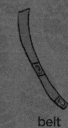
belt

ruler

sock

crescent moon

feather

canoe

pencil

Art by Nuño Alexandre Vieira

Rainy Day

There are six words (not pictures!) hidden in this scene.
Can you find CLOUDS, DAMP, PUDDLE, SHOWERS, STORMY, and WET?

Art by Kelly Kennedy

Say each tongue twister three times fast!

Wendy wearies of wet weather.

Patty plays in puddles.

Ren wore red rain boots.

The Magic Hat

Look what the magician found in his hat! See if you can find all the hidden objects.

ice-cream cone

toothbrush

saltshaker

artist's brush

banana

plunger

megaphone

paintbrush

baseball glove

eyeglasses

teacup

crown

shoe

saw

envelope

slice of pizza

lollipop

ring

saucepan

paint can

paper airplane

Art by Travis Foster

Each of these small scenes contains **6** hidden objects from the list below. Some objects are hidden in more than one scene. Can you find the **6** hidden objects in each scene?

Hidden Object List

The numbers tell you how many times each object is hidden.

button (2)

comb (4)

crescent moon (3)

dog bone (4)

heart (3)

magnet (3)

pencil (3)

ring (2)

slice of pizza (3)

snail (3)

spoon (4)

tennis ball (2)

BONUS
Two scenes contain the exact same set of hidden objects. Can you find that matching pair?

Art by Jana Curll

The Egg Factory

These rabbits are hard at work. Can you find all the hidden objects?

drinking straw

lollipop

ruler

wedge of orange

button

hockey stick

paper clip

harmonica

UFO

book

dustpan

ladle

waffle

mushroom

Art by Brian Michael Weaver

20

Hide It!

Can you hide this flower in your own Hidden Pictures drawing?

Hide It!   Can you hide this flower in your own Hidden Pictures drawing?

21

Wait for Me!

Can you find a path to help Blue Beetle reunite with his friends?

START

FINISH

Art by Mattia Cerato

Find and Doodle

Draw nets for Mike and Maria to use to catch butterflies. Then find the hidden bow tie, bowl, egg, fork, lollipop, peanut, raindrop, snake, and snowflake.

Rain, Rain, Here to Stay

Can you find at least 10 differences between these two pictures?

Art by Constanza Basaluzzo

How do birds fly in the rain?

Using wing-shield wipers

What do storm clouds wear in their hair?

Rainbows

Desert Egg Hunt

adhesive
bandage

pumpkin

toothbrush

hammer

boomerang

apple

fried egg

crown

skateboard

flying disk

26

Lizards like Easter egg hunts, too!
See if you can find all the hidden objects in the desert.

Art by Kyle Beckett

wedge of lemon

magnifying glass

domino

piece of popcorn

drinking straw

carrot

beach ball

button

bell

candle

mitten

The Bunny Bakery

Can you find the objects hidden throughout the kitchen?

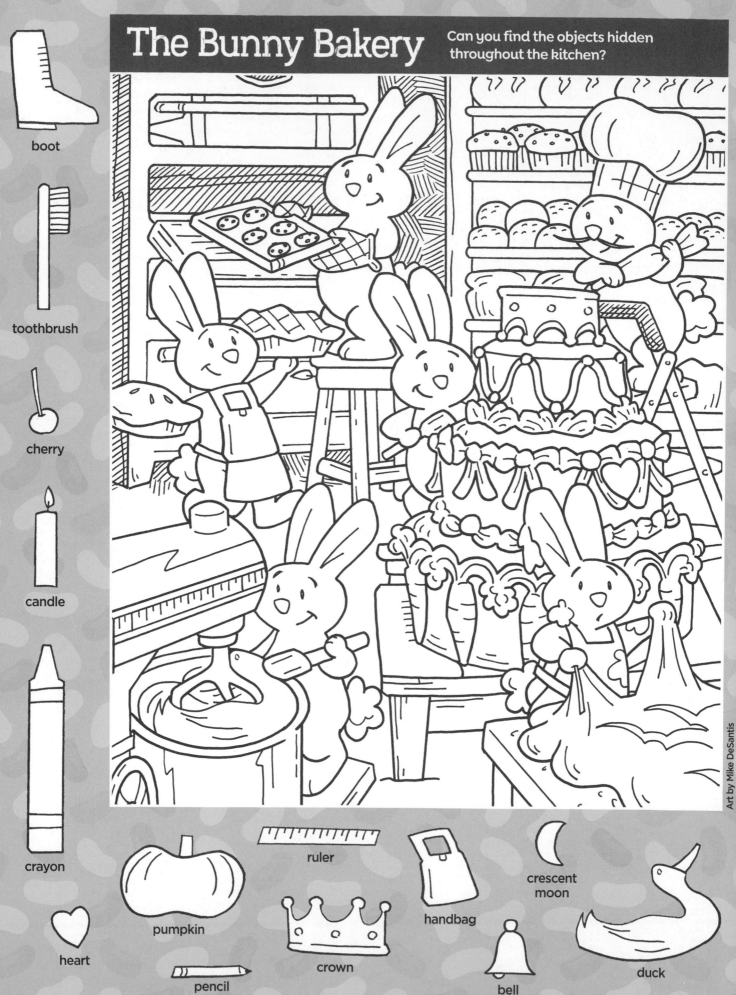

boot

toothbrush

cherry

candle

crayon

heart

pumpkin

pencil

ruler

crown

handbag

bell

crescent moon

duck

Art by Mike DeSantis

Queen's Quails

Can you find at least 12 differences between these two pictures?

Tic Tac Row

What do you think the boots in each row (horizontally, vertically, and diagonally) have in common?

Art by Kevin Zimmer

What color is rain?

Watercolor

What do you call a pair of rain boots in love?

Sole mates

Which things in this picture are silly? It's up to you!

Art by Josh Cleland

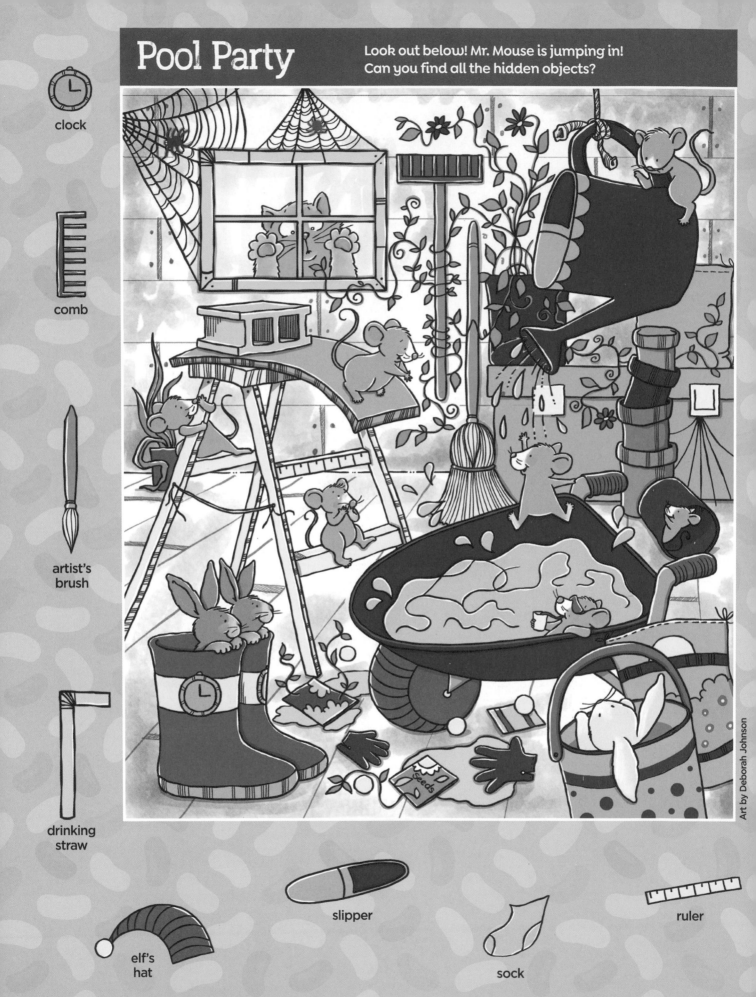

Pool Party

**Look out below! Mr. Mouse is jumping in!
Can you find all the hidden objects?**

clock

comb

artist's
brush

drinking
straw

elf's
hat

slipper

sock

ruler

Art by Deborah Johnson

Awesome Blossoms

Find four shamrocks, four butterflies, six dragonflies, and a purple beetle.

Art by Pintachan

33

Painting Pots

banana

comb

boomerang

magnifying glass

kite

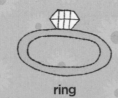
ring

sailboat

pine tree

carrot

fish

34

It's craft day at Springfield Elementary.
See if you can find all the hidden objects in the classroom.

ice-cream cone

baseball bat

pencil

envelope

needle

Art by Josh Cleland

wedge of cheese   mountains   ghost   ruler   magnet   bell

35

Leap into Spring

Knock, knock.
Who's there?
Bunny.
Bunny who?
Bunny thing is,
I've forgotten!

Knock, knock.
Who's there?
Garden.
Garden who?
Stop garden
the door!

cabbage

tomatoes

beets

squash

fried egg

fish

open book

slice of
pizza

seashell

It's gardening day, and all of the bunnies are helping.
Can you find the hidden objects in the garden?

pumpkin seeds

carrots

asparagus

Knock, knock.
Who's there?
Rosa.
Rosa who?
Rosa veggies
grow in
the garden.

Knock, knock.
Who's there?
Rabbit.
Rabbit who?
Rabbit carefully.
It's a present!

Art by Tamara Petrosino

ice-cream
bar

toothbrush

pencil

ruler

Spring Blossoms

There are eight words (not pictures!) hidden in this scene. Can you find BLOSSOM, BOOT, CITY, CLOUD, DOG, PINK, SPRING, and TREE?

40

Compost Heroes

Calvin, Josie, and Spencer are taking out the compost. See if you can find all the hidden objects.

golf club

pencil

candle

drinking straw

CARROTS

BEETS

Art by Mitch Mortimer

 ruler

envelope

cane

comb

 slice of pizza

teacup

 artist's brush

fork

 domino

heart

 ring

Each of these scenes contains 12 hidden objects, which are listed below. Find each object in one of the scenes, then cross it off the list.

Art by Brian Michael Weaver

ax	crescent moon	mallet	slice of pie
bottle	drinking straw	peanut	tack
bowling ball	fish	pineapple	toothbrush
button	flashlight	radish	wedge of cheese
cane	glove	sailboat	wedge of orange
crayon	harmonica	shoe	yo-yo

Visiting Grandma

The Francis family always has Easter dinner at Grandma's. Can you find all the hidden objects?

hockey stick

shovel

taco

fork

carrot

candle

toothbrush

ice-cream bar

slice of pie

book

fishing pole

key

slice of pizza

bell

Art by Kelly Kennedy

Can you hide this raindrop in your own Hidden Pictures drawing?

Easter Basket Hunt

Help these kids find their Easter baskets by following each path.

Art by Buff McAllister

Say each tongue twister three times fast!

Fifi finds five flowers.

Edgar ate exactly eight eggs.

Rapid rabbits run rampant.

Art by Brian Michael Weaver

47

Spring Is Here!

Can you find at least 10 differences between these two pictures?

How far is it from March to June?

Just a short spring

What did the tree say when spring came?

What a re-leaf!

What time of year is it best to use a trampoline?

In the springtime

How does a tree cheer for its favorite baseball team?

It roots for them.

Art by Jannie Ho

49

tack

teacup

kite

sock

magnet

balloon

baseball

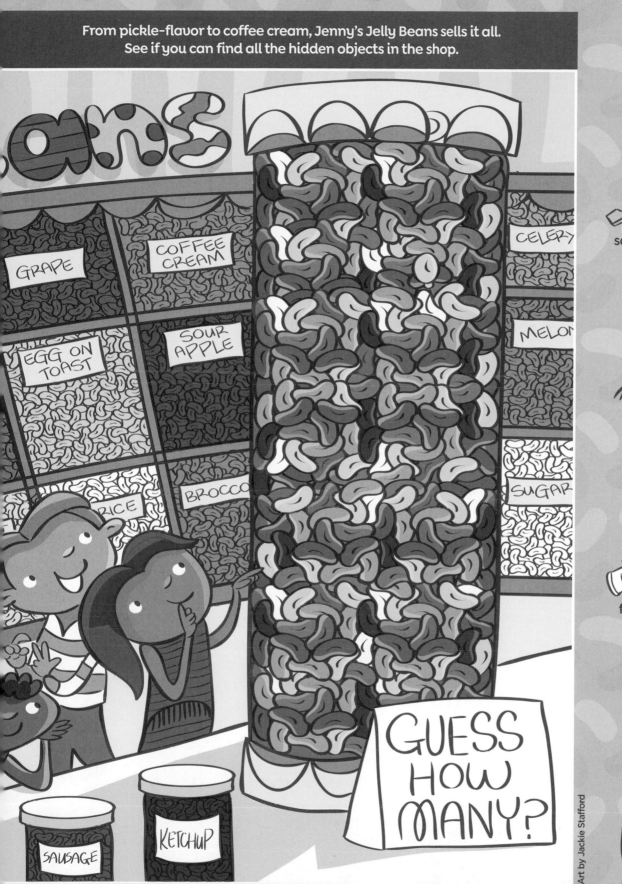

From pickle-flavor to coffee cream, Jenny's Jelly Beans sells it all.
See if you can find all the hidden objects in the shop.

GRAPE

COFFEE CREAM

CELERY

EGG ON TOAST

SOUR APPLE

MELON

RICE

BROCCO...

SUGAR

GUESS HOW MANY?

SAUSAGE

KETCHUP

Art by Jackie Stafford

screwdriver

comb

flashlight

hot dog

crescent moon

heart

dog bone

City Nesters

Can you find all the hidden objects in these nests and the city down below?

baseball bat

glove

nail

drinking straw

umbrella

fish

banana

comb

pencil

fork

bell

envelope

mitten

teacup

slice of pizza

heart

paper clip

Art by Kyle Beckett

Salad Assemblers

Can you find at least 10 differences between these two pictures?

Art by Pat N. Lewis

Six by Six

Each of these small scenes contains **6** hidden objects from the list below. Some objects are hidden in more than one scene. Can you find the **6** hidden objects in each scene?

Hidden Object List

The numbers tell you how many times each object is hidden.

boomerang (4)

crescent moon (2)

crown (3)

fork (4)

magnifying glass (3)

pencil (4)

saltshaker (2)

teacup (3)

toothbrush (3)

umbrella (2)

wedge of orange (3)

yo-yo (3)

BONUS
Two scenes contain the exact same set of hidden objects. Can you find that matching pair?

Art by Kelly Kennedy

Springy Fun

Boing! Boing! Look at them go!
See if you can find the hidden objects.

Art by Viviana Garofoli

needle

banana

paper clip

lollipop

bell

artist's brush

pencil

button

Hen Frenzy

Can you find the goat? Can you also find 12 hidden eggs?

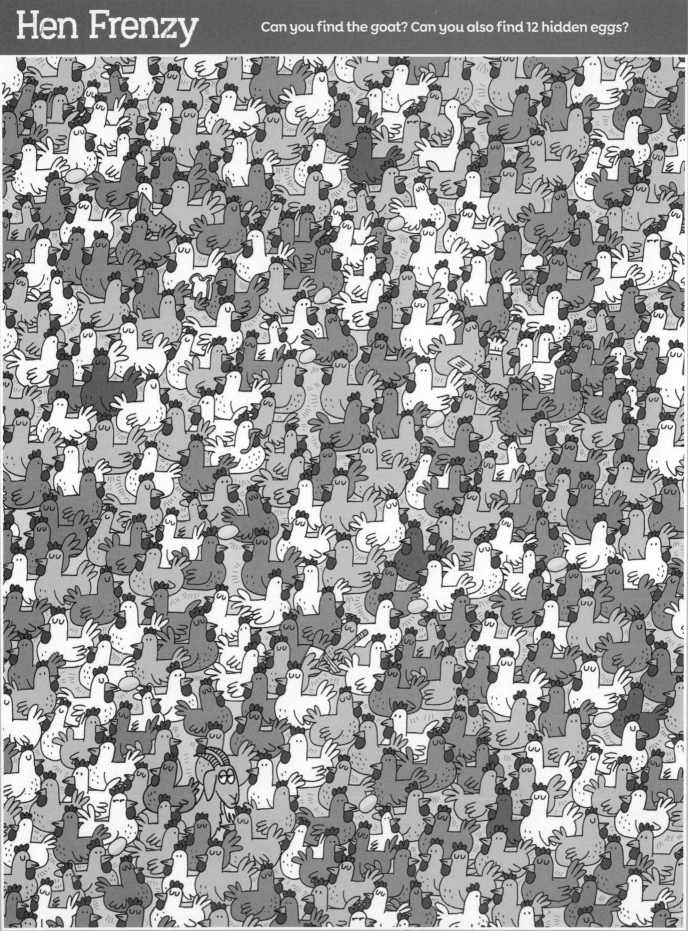

Art by Travis Foster

Forest Festivities

crescent
moon

ruler

candy
cane

golf club

bell

crown   cinnamon bun   baseball   adhesive
bandage   snake

mitten

bowling pin

toothbrush

ice-cream cone

slice of pizza

Art by Tamara Petrosino

comb

birdcage

waffle

envelope

teacup

59

Spring Cleanup

cane

thimble

sailboat

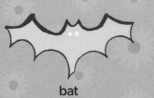

bat

toothbrush

spoon

ice-cream
cone

cat

olive

Art by Brian Michael Weaver

fish

heart

magnet

comb

Easter Village

Art by Jana Curll

Otter Slide

Art by Kelly Kennedy

umbrella

bat

artist's brush

fork

boot

horseshoe

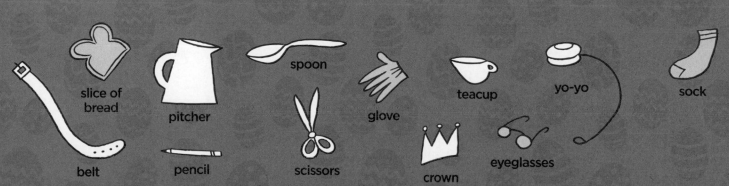

slice of bread

pitcher

spoon

scissors

glove

teacup

crown

eyeglasses

yo-yo

sock

belt

pencil

65

Tic Tac Row

What do the umbrellas in each row (horizontally, vertically, and diagonally) have in common?

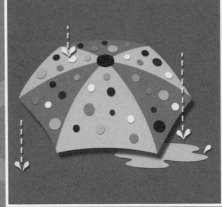

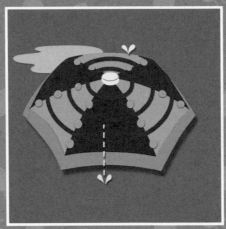

Art by Judith Moffat

What goes up when rain comes down?

Umbrellas

What did the raindrop say when it fell?

"Oops! I dripped."

Let's Decorate!

Which things in this picture are silly? It's up to you!

Art by Julissa Mora

Say each tongue twister three times fast!

Paisley picked purple paint.

The sun shines on Sunday.

Esther enjoys every Easter.

Let it Grow

Rabbit and Raccoon are watering their plants. Can you find the hidden objects?

mushroom

magnet

peanut

book

crayon

spoon

bell

toothbrush

slice of pizza

Art by Mary Sullivan

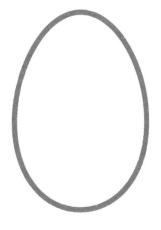

seashell

Iron

snowman

golf tee

snow cone

butter knife

tooth

fish

match

horn

piece of popcorn

teacup

open book

ruler

It's always springtime in the indoor butterfly garden.
See if you can find all the hidden objects in the exhibit.

wedge of cheese

fishhook

scissors

saltshaker

sock

toy top

slice of pie

artist's brush

arrow   crown   sailboat   heart   needle

Art by Laura Ferraro Close

Searching for Eggs

Can you find at least 10 differences between these two pictures?

Greenhouse Growth

bird

frog

teacup

butterfly

light bulb

snail

dog's bone

hammer

doughnut

All of the plants in Gregor's Greenhouse are green and growing.
Can you find the hidden objects among the plants?

mouse

paintbrush

fork

seahorse

banana

worm

key

crayon

scissors

Art by Jim Paillot

75

Perfect Puddle

Alyssa and Forest love rainy days.
See if you can find the hidden objects.

game piece

domino

light bulb

broccoli

heart

fish

spoon

wedge of lemon

test tube

slice of pie

drumstick

ice-cream cone

Art by Dana Regan

Shoe Shopping

Can you find at least 12 differences between these two pictures?

Rainbow Chicks

beet juice →

You Need
* Hard-boiled eggs
* Grape juice or other natural dye
* Mayonnaise
* Mustard
* Olives
* Carrots

1. Peel hard-boiled eggs. Cut them in half. Put the yolks in a bowl. Cover the bowl and put it into the fridge.

2. Put the whites into a cup full of grape juice or another natural dye. Soak them overnight in the fridge, then set them on a paper towel to dry.

← water from boiled red cabbage

3. For each yolk in the bowl, add two teaspoons of mayonnaise and one teaspoon of mustard. Mash with a fork.

4. Spoon the yolk mixture into the egg whites. Use olive bits for eyes and carrots for beaks and legs.

grape juice →

78

RACE to the Flower

A Game for Two Players

You Need

* Small box
* Colored paper
* Cardboard tube
* Velcro dots
* Cardboard
* Markers
* Cardstock
* Penny
* Glue
* Scissors

 1 Cover a small box with colored paper. Trace the end of a cardboard tube on the top of the box. Cut out the circle. Cover the cardboard tube with paper, then glue one end into the box.

2 Attach the loop side of Velcro dots to the tube.

3 For ladybugs, cut two ovals from cardboard. Cover each with paper of a different color. Add details with markers. Attach the hook side of a Velcro dot to the back of each ladybug.

 4 Cut a large flower from colored paper. Decorate it with markers and paper. Cut slits at the top of the tube and slide the flower into them.

5 Cover a penny with paper, making the two sides match the two ladybug colors.

To Play

Players take turns flipping the penny. If the penny lands with your ladybug color facing up, move up one dot. If it doesn't, it's the other player's turn. The first bug to reach the flower wins!

DRIP POTS

You Need
- ★ Clear sealer
- ★ Paintbrush
- ★ Terra-cotta pot
- ★ Acryllic paint
- ★ Water

1. Paint clear sealer onto the inside and outside of a terra-cotta pot. Let it dry.

2. Paint the outside of the pot with white acrylic paint. Let it dry.

3. Mix another color of paint with a few drops of water so that it drips like milk.

4. Place the pot upside down on a covered surface. Drip the watery paint onto the pot. Let it dry.

5. Add a coat of clear sealer.

Veggie Bugs

Ask an adult for help with anything sharp.

Try different ingredients, such as turkey slices or hummus.

You Need
* Cucumbers
* Tomatoes
* Celery
* Olives
* Chives
* Cream cheese or hummus

1 Cut cucumbers into circles. Slice tomatoes in half. Cut celery into two-inch logs. Chop olives into small squares. Trim chives into one-inch stalks.

2 Spread cream cheese or hummus onto celery with a butter knife.

3 Place cucumber and tomato on celery log. Place chives behind tomato (for antennae). Add cream cheese to help steady it.

4 Dab cream cheese on tomato for eyes. Then put olive squares onto the cream cheese.

Easter Basket

You Need
* Tissue box
* Colored paper
* Glue
* Scissors
* Metal fasteners
* Ribbon
* Tape
* Easter grass

 Cut the top off a square tissue box. Cover it with colored paper. Make an egg out of paper. Glue it to the box.

 Poke two holes in the box. Use metal fasteners to attach a ribbon as a handle. Tape down the ends of the fasteners. Add Easter grass.

Egg Hunt Matching Game

A Game for Two or More Players

You Need
* Craft foam
* Scissors
* Glue

 Cut an even number of eggs from craft foam.

 Decorate them with craft foam so that each egg has a match.

 Hide the eggs around your house or in your backyard. The player who finds the most matching pairs wins.

Colorful Confetti Eggs

You Need

- ★ Butter knife
- ★ Eggs
- ★ Small bowl
- ★ Paint or crayons
- ★ Paintbrush
- ★ Paper
- ★ Confetti
- ★ Scissors
- ★ Tissue paper
- ★ Glue

1 Use the butter knife to make a small hole in the bottom of the egg.

2 Empty the egg into a small bowl. Rinse the inside of the egg with water. Let dry.

3 Decorate the eggshells with paint or crayons.

4 Roll a piece of paper to create a funnel. Place the small end inside the hole. Pour the confetti through the funnel.

5 Cut a small piece of tissue paper. Glue it over the hole. Let dry.

Surprise!
Gently crush the eggs over a friend's head

Eggshells filled with confetti, called cascarones, are a Mexican tradition during Easter.

kiwi

strawberries

star fruit

cantaloupe

raspberries

mango

pineapple

kiwi

WRAP 'N' ROLL

Transform fruit into tasty spring rolls.

bananas

You Need
- ★ Rice paper
- ★ Water
- ★ Pastry brush
- ★ Cutting board
- ★ Fruit

Ask an adult for help with anything sharp.

1 Dunk a piece of rice paper into water to soften it.

2 Spread out the rice paper on a cutting board. Brush more water onto any stiff spots.

3 Place thinly sliced fruit just above the center of the rice paper. Leave room around the fruit.

4 Fold down the rice paper at the top.

5 Fold in the sides.

6 Roll the rest of the paper around the fruit.

blackberries

strawberries

kiwi

strawberries

Dip them into a mixture of honey and lemon juice.

You Need
* ★ Corrugated cardboard
* ★ Colored paper
* ★ Yarn
* ★ Pencil
* ★ Dyed eggshells
* ★ Glue
* ★ Scissors
* ★ Tape

Easter Mosaics

 1 Cover corrugated cardboard with colored paper. Tape a yarn hanger to the back.

 2 With a pencil, lightly draw a simple shape on the paper, such as an egg or a cross.

 3 Fill the shape by gluing on pieces of clean, dyed eggshells.

 4 Add a paper border as a decoration.

stir it up

Lavender Lift

lavender sprig

lemon-lime seltzer

Berry Blitz

Orange Spritz

orange slices

ginger seltzer

mint leaves

lemon and lime slices

plain seltzer

basil leaves

berries

Ask an adult for help with anything sharp.

You Need
* Baking soda
* Flour
* White glue
* Water
* Food coloring
* Plastic eggs

Sidewalk-Chalk Easter Eggs

1. In a bowl, mix together 1 cup of baking soda, 1 cup of flour, ½ cup of white glue, and 3 tablespoons of water.

2. Divide the mixture into several cups. Mix a few drops of food coloring into each.

3. Press the mixture into plastic eggs, filling both halves. Close them.

4. Let them dry for a day. Remove the chalk from the eggs, and let it dry until it hardens.

Answers

▼ Pages 2–3

▼ Page 4

▼ Page 5

▼ Pages 6–7

▼ Page 8

▼ Page 9

Answers

▼ Pages 10-11

▼ Pages 14-15

▼ Page 16

▼ Page 17

▼ Pages 18–19

Answers

▼ Page 20

▼ Page 22

▼ Page 23

▼ Pages 24–25

▼ Pages 26–27

▼ Page 28

▼ Page 29

▼ Page 30

Red Stripe Green Toe Polka Dots	Red Stripe Handles	Red Stripe Animal Pattern Yellow Sole
Buckle Green Toe	Buckle Handles Polka Dots Yellow Sole	Buckle Animal Pattern
Green Stripe Green Toe Yellow Sole	Green Stripe Handles	Green Stripe Animal Pattern Polka Dots

Answers

▼ Page 32

▼ Page 33

▼ Pages 34–35

▼ Pages 38–39

▼ Page 40

Answers

▼ Page 41

▼ Pages 42–43

▼ Page 44

▼ Page 46

▼ Page 47

▼ Pages 48–49

▼ Pages 50–51

Answers

▼ Page 52

▼ Page 53

▼ Pages 54–55

▼ Page 56

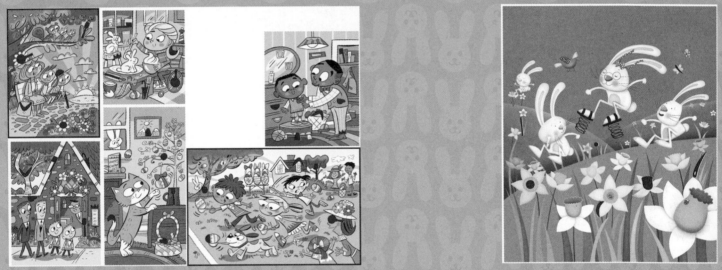

▼ Page 57

▼ Pages 58–59

Answers

▼ Pages 62–63

▼ Page 64

▼ Page 65

▼ Page 66

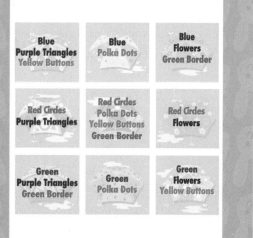

Blue **Purple Triangles** **Yellow Buttons**	**Blue** **Polka Dots**	**Blue** **Flowers** **Green Border**
Red Circles **Purple Triangles**	**Red Circles** **Polka Dots** **Yellow Buttons** **Green Border**	**Red Circles** **Flowers**
Green **Purple Triangles** **Green Border**	**Green** **Polka Dots**	**Green** **Flowers** **Yellow Buttons**

▼ Page 68

▼ Pages 70–71

▼ Pages 72–73

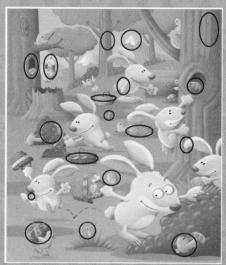

▼ Pages 74–75

▼ Page 76

▼ Page 77

Published by Highlights Press
815 Church Street
Honesdale, Pennsylvania 18431
ISBN: 978-1-64472-914-4
Manufactured in Shenzhen, Guangdong, China
Mfg. 11/2022
First edition
Visit our website at Highlights.com.
10 9 8 7 6 5 4 3 2 1

Cover art by Erica Salcedo
Craft photos by Guy Cali Associates, Inc., except Race to the Flower (page 79) by Hank Schneider,
background (page 79) by iStock/Piotr Krzeslak, and background (page 83) by iStock/J33P312.
Craft illustrations (pages 78 and 80) by Mike Lowery.

Easter Egg Tips: To make an Easter egg garland, punch out a small hole at the top of each egg and thread a long piece of string or ribbon through the holes on every egg. Ask an adult for help with anything sharp.

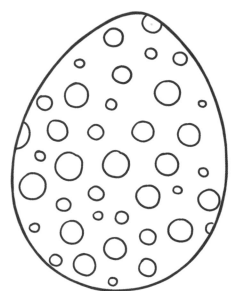

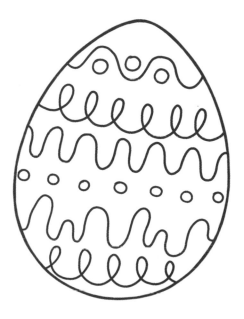

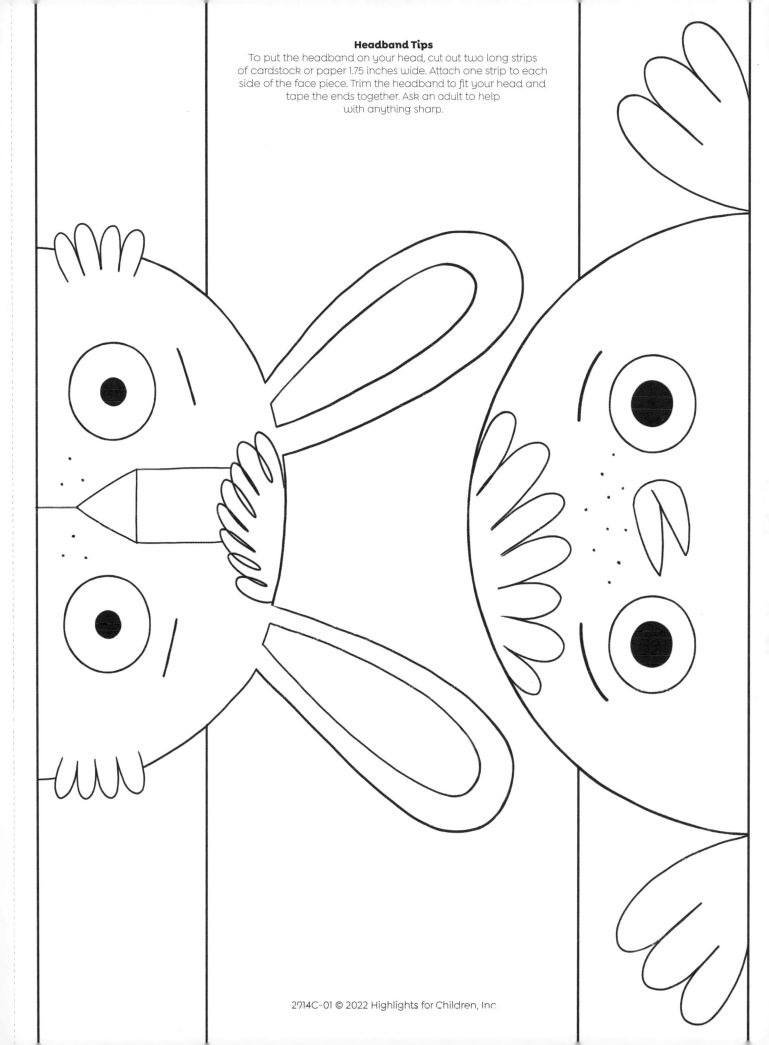

Headband Tips
To put the headband on your head, cut out two long strips of cardstock or paper 1.75 inches wide. Attach one strip to each side of the face piece. Trim the headband to fit your head and tape the ends together. Ask an adult to help with anything sharp.

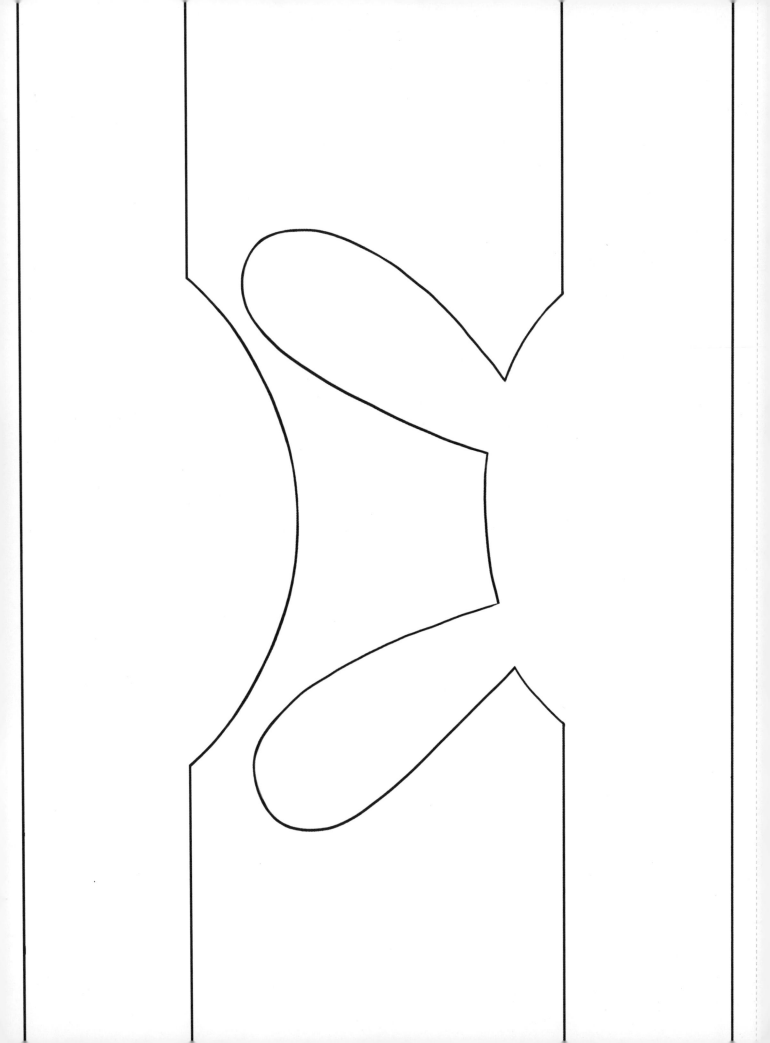

Egg Hunt

Bloom

Happy Easter!

Egg Hunt

SPRING